Going to Work SCHOOL EDITION · Going to Work SCHOOL EDITION · Going to Work SCHOOL EDITION · Going to Work SCHOOL EDITION · Going to Work SCHOOL EDITION · Going to Work SCHOOL EDITION · Going to Work SCHOOL EDITION · Going to Work SCHOOL EDITION · Going to Work SCHOOL EDITION · Going to Work SCHOOL EDITION

Going To Work
SCHOOL EDITION

Librarians

Buddy BOOKS
Going To Work

ABDO
Publishing Company

A Buddy **Book by**
Julie Murray

VISIT US AT
www.abdopublishing.com

Published by ABDO Publishing Company, 8000 West 78th Street, Edina, Minnesota 55439.

Printed in the United States of America, North Mankato, Minnesota.
022010
092010

 PRINTED ON RECYCLED PAPER

Coordinating Series Editor: Rochelle Baltzer
Editor: Sarah Tieck
Contributing Editors: Heidi M.D. Elston, Megan M. Gunderson, BreAnn Rumsch, Marcia Zappa
Graphic Design: Maria Hosley
Cover Photograph: *Shutterstock*: Lisa F. Young.
Interior Photographs/Illustrations: *AP Photo*: Andy Wong (p. 30); *Corbis*: © Gabe Palmer (p. 15); *Getty Images*: Evans/Three Lions (p. 27); Michael P. Goecke (pp. 5, 19); *iStockphoto*: ©iStockphoto.com/aldomurillo (p. 7), ©iStockphoto.com/Jbryson (p. 23), ©iStockphoto.com/RichVintage (p. 13),©iStockphoto.com/track5 (pp. 11, 17, 29), ©iStockphoto.com/wynnter (p. 25); *Shutterstock*: Rob Marmion (pp. 21, 23), Dmitriy Shironosov (p. 5), wow (p. 8), Lisa F. Young (p. 9).

Library of Congress Cataloging-in-Publication Data

Murray, Julie, 1969-
  Librarians / Julie Murray.
     p. cm. -- (Going to work. School edition)
  ISBN 978-1-61613-506-5
  1. School librarians--Juvenile literature. 2. School libraries--Juvenile literature. 3. Instructional materials centers--Juvenile literature. 4. Library science--Vocational guidance--Juvenile literature. I. Title.
  z682.4.s34M87 2011
  020.23--dc22
                                                                    2009050817

Contents

People at Work

Going to work is an important part of life. At work, people use their skills to complete tasks and earn money.

There are many different types of workplaces. Schools, factories, and offices are all workplaces.

Some librarians work in schools. They help students and teachers find **resources** to aid learning. This is honorable work.

School libraries are a resource for learners and teachers. Today, they contain more than just books!

5

Helping Out

School librarians are sometimes called media specialists. They work in school libraries, or media centers.

School librarians may work part-time or full-time. They manage a school library's books and other resources. They also order new books and supplies for the library.

Students can check out books and more from their school library.

Media in a school library may include CDs, DVDs, and magazines.

Did You Know?

Students use library computers to play educational games and research subjects.

School libraries serve students of all ages. Students visit libraries to check out books and use computers.

School librarians teach students and teachers about libraries. They show them how to use library resources.

Librarians often suggest books for students to read.

Working Together

School librarians work with many people. Students go to the library to use its **resources**. Teachers and other school workers also visit the library. Librarians help them find the **information** they need.

Each library has a reference section, where reference books are shelved. Reference books cannot be checked out. Students use them in the library.

College Days

To become a librarian, a person must have a college **degree**. Most librarians must also attend graduate school. There, they earn advanced degrees, such as master's degrees or doctorates.

To earn a degree, librarian students study library science and **information** science. Many also study education. This prepares them to work in schools.

After library students complete college, they are ready to begin work.

Information science is the system of gathering, storing, and organizing information.

Did You Know?

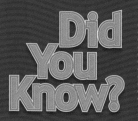
In their classes, librarian students learn about organizing information. They study how to use reference systems and help library users. They also learn about computers and the Internet.

Before being hired, a librarian must get a license from his or her state. Each state has different requirements.

Librarians need strong listening skills.
This helps them work with people.

A Look Inside

School libraries contain many types of **resources**. There are books, newspapers, magazines, journals, CDs, DVDs, and computers.

Librarians make sure the school library resources stay organized. To do this, they use the Dewey decimal system. It sorts resources by numbers so people can find them easily.

Librarians sort books and other items onto carts and shelves. This helps keep the library running smoothly.

Teaching Teachers

Sometimes, teachers need help finding **resources** to plan lessons. School librarians know about many resources. So, they can offer helpful suggestions.

Librarians use computers to look up books and check them out to teachers and students.

Reaching Students

School librarians teach students skills they may not learn in the classroom. They teach them how to find **information**. Librarians also show students how to use computers and the Internet.

Computers are one of many learning tools in a library.

21

School libraries create opportunities for students. Students can use resources they may not have at home. And, learning how to research subjects is a useful life skill.

For many students, school librarians help build a love of reading. Librarians read to groups of children. They also help students find books to read for fun.

Librarians, teachers, and parents read to students in the library. And, students may practice reading out loud to strengthen their reading skills.

HISTORY LESSON

Today, people can borrow books for free from libraries. But long ago, there were no public libraries. And, most people couldn't afford to buy books.

Then in 1731, members of the Junto Club bought books to share. These books were just for club members. Still, this is considered the first library. Soon, the idea of sharing books caught on.

Benjamin Franklin started the Junto Club in 1727. The group met every Friday night to discuss important ideas.

Did You Know?

Benjamin Franklin was a student at Boston Latin School. He later became a famous printer, scientist, and inventor.

The first school libraries likely started with the first public schools. Teachers collected books for their students to read.

The first U.S. public school is Boston Latin School in Massachusetts. It opened in 1635. Students still attend this school today!

Years ago, students mostly used books. Today, they use many more learning resources.

Helpful Workers

School librarians do many important tasks. They **manage** library **resources**. They help students and teachers. And, they aid learning. School librarians do meaningful work that benefits the community!

School librarians are an important part of their communities.

The School News

First Lady of Books

Laura Bush was First Lady from 2001 to 2009. Before that, she had been a teacher and a librarian in Texas schools. Laura used her job as First Lady to share her love of reading.  She created a charity to give money to libraries and to help kids read.

Honoring Libraries

October is International School Library Month. It honors school libraries and librarians.

Important Words

degree a title given by a college to its students for completing their studies. An advanced degree, such as a master's or a doctorate, is earned by completing graduate school after college.

information (ihn-fuhr-MAY-shuhn) knowledge obtained from learning or studying something.

license (LEYE-suhnts) a paper or a card showing that someone is allowed to do something by law.

manage to look after or make decisions about.

media ways of sharing information, especially to large groups of people. Radio, television, newspapers, and magazines are examples of media.

reference (REH-fuhrnts) a work, such as a book, containing useful facts.

research to carefully study a subject in order to learn facts about it.

resources a supply of something. A library's resources include books, magazines, CDs, DVDs, and computers.

Web Sites

To learn more about librarians, visit ABDO Publishing Company online. Web sites about librarians are featured on our Book Links page. These links are routinely monitored and updated to provide the most current information available.

www.abdopublishing.com

Index